Two Poets
and a Squirrel

By Morris Corn, Ed.D and Olivia Michelle
Illustrated by Kelsey DeVries and Nate Frank

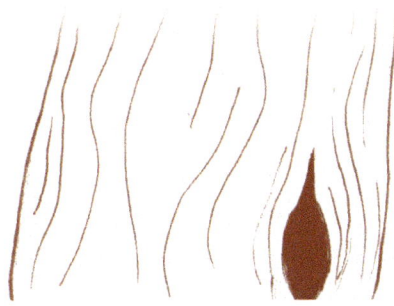

Dedicated to Ruth Leah — my wife —
whose love is more than any aspiring teacher deserves.

THE STORY BEGINS...

We all have a poem inside of us that can be shared and bring us together, across generations.

The story begins ... Friday night was an evening for the Corn family to get together to celebrate the start of the Sabbath. This included grandparents, parents, and twelve grandchildren.

It came to pass that a poetry contest between the young and old was born. Everyone loved the poems and the poets were applauded.

A grandchild who stood out was a seven-year-old little girl named Olivia. She was matched against her grandfather, Morris. Grandma Ruth, fair and unafraid, was tasked with judging the contest and declaring a winner. Week after week, Grandpa Morris earned a tie, at best, but usually Olivia won out. Olivia was met with cheers and applause.

After Grandma and Grandpa moved to Florida, Olivia and Grandpa continued to write to each other. Distance did not stop them from sharing their love of poetry and their connection that grew out of it.

This book is a collection of their poems, written over a period of 15 years.

Every poem was written to connect with both love and humor.

FROM THE AUTHORS

I have loved poetry since college.

Once I graduated, working as a new teacher with a class of eighteen 6th graders, I realized the power of poetry as a tool to connect in the classroom.

I struggled to get my students' attention, until I read them the Lewis Carroll poem, "You Are Old, Father William":

> "You are old, Father William," the young man said,
> "And your hair has become very white;
> And yet you incessantly stand on your head-
> Do you think, at your age, it is right?"
> "In my youth," Father William replied to his son,
> "I feared it might injure the brain;
> But now that I am perfectly sure I have none,
> Why, I do it again and again."

The kids all laughed and I had their attention! What fun! Welcome to the power of poetry. I went on to share poetry with my children and grandchildren. It was a way to play and learn with them. My granddaughter, Olivia, loved it so much that she began to write poetry at an early age. Writing poems for each other, we used wordplay to learn, communicate, share, laugh, create, and connect. And that joy spilled over onto the whole family. Our shared passion for poetry, and the fun and silliness that we created with words and ideas, enabled me to nurture a bond with my granddaughter that transcended time, age, and physical distance.

This book is our collection of fun. I hope you enjoy it as well and that it allows you to play and connect with the people you love.

My introduction to poetry began with my grandfather, Dr. Morris Corn. One of my earliest poetry memories is listening to Grandpa Morris recite a verse of his favorite poem, "The Walrus and the Carpenter," by Lewis Caroll.

My grandfather, a highly talented poet and writer himself, not only encouraged my passion, but also engaged in it with me. Every Friday, after our family Shabbat dinner, he and I would face off in a poetry contest. I usually won; however, Grandma Ruth was judging, and I was in elementary school, so I suspect some preferential treatment might have been at play.

When my grandparents moved to Florida full-time, Grandpa Morris and I continued our tradition by sending poems back and forth over email. My grandfather's constant encouragement, advice, and genuine appreciation for my poetry over the years gave me the confidence to continue to write as I grew older, and to submit my work to various competitions.

Now, I am a recent college graduate and poetry remains an extremely important part of my life, connecting me to my grandfather in ways that I treasure deeply. I am so honored to have my poetry in this book beside his and am so excited to share our passion with fellow poetry-lovers.

Olivia Michelle

THE SQUIRREL
Olivia | Age 10

I was sitting
At the table
When outside
I saw a squirrel
On a tree
It jumped
Onto a branch
That was thin.
The branch shook
Under the squirrel
   Up and
      Down
   Up and
      Down.

I covered my eyes
I was sure
It would fall.
BUT
It did not.
It scampered
Off the branch
And went
To a higher one.

The same thing
Happened.
Again.
And again.
And again.
Until it fell.
It was
A long
   Way
      Down.
   BUT
      It did not die.

The squirrel tried again.
Because a squirrel
Knows
Not
To
Give
Up.
Even though
It's just a squirrel.

ODE TO A GRANDPA
Olivia | Age 10

Morris Corn, a wonderful man,
If he can't play checkers, no one can!
A great personality lies within him,
His love for everyone spills over the brim!

He has the kindest heart on Earth,
He has been loved since the day of his birth.
Morris Corn has an extremely brilliant mind,
The way he writes poetry is one of a kind!

He is honest, and that is true,
No matter what, he's truthful to you.
You can feel his love from miles away,
About him there are so many nice things to say!

So as we celebrate, please remember,
That our 80-year-old friend and family member,
Will always have overflowing kindness for all,
So let's do him a favor, make his 80th birthday a ball!

OLIVIA'S ALMOST 11
Grandpa Morris

Olivia's ten years old right now
And entering 5th grade
So many happy times and memories were made.

Olivia's almost 11
For 2 months she must wait
But the day is sure to come
There's no need for a debate.

November 14, 2010
is the lucky day
But when she finally gets there
She's still not there to stay…

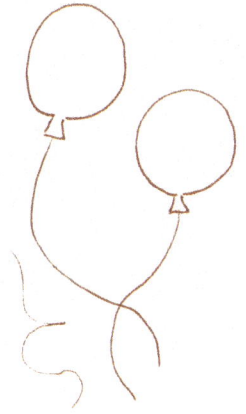

Olivia Michelle's almost 12
Well, not quite
One whole year has to go round
Before one-two's in sight

But one-one is a big deal
And Olivia's getting ready
It's almost time to celebrate
Start throwing confetti.

WHY DOES MY TEACHER HATE ME?
Olivia | Age 12

Why does my teacher hate me?
I really don't understand
I only hid the drumsticks
From the 6th grade band.

It can't be from spilling soda
On her new computer
Or riding into science class
On my electric scooter.

She can't be mad about the time
I was late to every class
Or the day we had the test
And I said I'll pass.

So really, I have no idea
What I'm doing wrong
Maybe she's just grumpy
So I'll go along.

THE BABYSITTER
Olivia | Age 12

Yesterday I was employed
To sit for little Jen.
I bet her Mom will ask me back
Over and over again.

I fed her lots of candy bars
What a sparkle in her eye!
I taught her many useful skills
Like how to cheat and lie!

We played tag in the sitting room
I showed her how to break a lamp
When I taught her how to prank call
We might've signed her up for camp.

We practiced skating in the kitchen
By pouring flour on the floor
We played baseball in the house
There aren't windows anymore.

When her Mom came back
She was so shocked
She couldn't even speak.
I guess I'm just amazing
And so much more than
   what they seek.

MY FATHER'S CREDIT CARD

Olivia | Age 10

I found my father's credit card
Inside his drawer with socks
And that day I realized
A credit card really rocks.

I got a new video game
And it was for free
The guy just scanned the credit card
And gave it back to me!

I got a baseball and a bat
With that credit card
I also got a college book
But it was way too hard.

And best of all
I got my Dad
A thank you card from me
For helping kids make this great discovery.

So that's why I don't understand
When our bill came here
My dad got REALLY REALLY mad
And I'm grounded for a year.

LITTLE JAMIE'S BLANKET
Olivia | Age 13

Little Jamie had a blanket
It was pink and fringed with lace
And she always had it with her
Any time and any place

She brought it to the playground
To the market, to her school
She even loved it so much
She tried to bring it in the pool!

All while this was happening
The little girl was growing older
She was getting taller
Getting smarter
Getting bolder

One day she saw her blanket
Just sitting on her bed
And realized how long it was
Since thoughts of it filled her head.

Jamie has a blanket
It is pink and fringed with lace
And though it's not always with her
In her heart, it has a place.

GRANDPA MORRIS'S FAMOUS HANDSHAKE
Grandpa Morris

Grandpa Morris's famous handshake
Is known throughout the world
Everyone knows it's worth
It's worth its weight in gold

It is recommended for the young, not for the old
It's the secret of how to become forever bold

A firm grasp — you'll hear a silent gasp
Eye contact — be sharp — is part of the art

Turning a little blue is the first clue
Firm your grip — If you want to leave a lasting impression
That completes the lesson

Young or old, you'll always be remembered
Grandpa Morris's Famous Handshake, by any other name,
Will always, always be the same

LUCK
Olivia | Age 10

What is luck?
Will it be there for me
When I fail a test, or get stung by a bee?

Is it a four leaf clover
Laying in the grass
Or a burst of light
That hits me when I pass?

Is luck a thing? Or something you can't see?
Is it something to own
Or something to be?

So what is luck?
When does it appear
Is it something to love
Or something to fear?

Luck's complicated as you can see
It will always be a mystery.

POEM NUMBER 3A
(I'M STILL WAITING)
Grandpa Morris

I'm still waiting for a poem that hasn't yet come my dear
Maybe it was lost, my memory isn't that clear
Or it could be that the day was long
And something else came along

Whatever the reason, please send a new one to hear
And relieve the heartfelt emptiness I bear
Maybe it's because I'm old and have a little cold
"You can't recall," I'm told

We know, we know, out of mind and out in the cold
My thoughts are many, if I was short and stubby

You might visualize an image caught
Or if my hair were down to the floor
Would that be a better décor?

WHATEVER, let's be real
Get that pencil sharpened, my sweet
And make #3 a real treat.

POEM NUMBER 3B
(I'M SORRY YOU HAD TO WAIT)

Olivia | Age 12

Grandpa,
I'm sorry you've felt you had to wait
I'm sure it wasn't much fun
You've sent me many many requests
For at least poem number one.

But if you recall, we were on the phone
Now try really hard to remember,
I said not that I'd send you the poems,
That I'd show you when you came in September!

You be the judge, Grandma!

POEM #1
Olivia | Age 12

As I sit here at my desk
I can assure you it's not fun
'Cause I can't think of anything
For Poem #1.

I have not one single idea
Don't have any rhyme
Grandpa needs this before he leaves
I DON'T HAVE ANY TIME!

So now I'm staring at the screen
Just drowning in despair
Why can't I think of ANYTHING?
IT JUST ISN'T FAIR!

I DON'T HAVE A POEM, OKAY?
I hope that's understood!
Hey wait, this IS a poem!
And I think it's pretty good!

POEM #2
Olivia | Age 12

The world can be
Such an ugly place
A dark gloominess over
Every inch of its space.

Until I get home
Snuggled safe in my bed
That's when the visions start up in my head.

The grassy green meadows
All covered in flowers
Filled up with fairies and magical powers

Bright colors are bursting
The bees buzz in tune
It's unspeakable joy
That nothing can ruin.

Children are laughing
Playing tag with the breeze
The sky's brilliant blue
Everyone is at ease.

Then the sun comes around
And lets down its beams
The stairs that take us away from our dreams

But I climb right back up
Don't put up a fight
'Cause I know I'll be back
Tomorrow night.

MY LITTLE COMPANION
Olivia | Age 7

I have a little companion
on each other we rely
sometimes we have to say no to each other
but we don't like to deny.

My companion is always joyful
a real nice person to see
I have a very good time with her
do you think she has a good time with me?

I'll tell you one more thing about her
and I'll tell you in a whisper
my really joyful companion
is also my little sister.

BUILD ME UP
Cayla Madison | Olivia's "Little Companion"

After all you do is try to build me up
You end up letting me down
Don't ever think
What you do matters to me
No matter
How well you do things
I won't care
I don't appreciate you
Stop saying
That I need you here
I just want to say
You aren't purposeful in my life
No one can convince me that
You mean the world to me

Now read the poem from the bottom up to hear the truth!

AN ODE BY GRANDPA

Grandpa Morris

Grandpa Morris, some say, who is never serious,
Whose jokes are delirious
Has a way with words, that some say,
Are for the birds.

You scratch your head because
You can't remember what he said
One must wonder, did he ever get out of bed?

Nothing is against his will
One must wonder if he'll ever keep still.

Having said all that, don't despair
You'll have to repeat yourself
A hundred times my dear.

He can't recall
His memory has taken a fall
It's just a short stint
Grandpa Morris can take a hint.

BRAGGY BART

Olivia | Age 14

There once was a little boy named Bart
Who was as sweet as could be
But he had one big problem
That all but he could see.

Bart bragged about everything!
No matter how big or small
Could be shoes, or ships, or sealing wax
He bragged about it all!

It got pretty tiring
He went on all day!
Soon it got so bad
That with him, no one would play.

This made poor Bart very sad
He did not know what he'd done
Until a little friend of his
Saw he was never having fun

She said, "Oh, Bart, I'm sorry.
I wish that you could play!
If only you didn't brag so much
You could join us every day!"

Bart, delighted, shouted out
"Why didn't you say?
If I'd known that I was bragging
I would've stopped right away!"

So from that day on, Bart didn't brag again
Which, may I say, was quite relieving
To all his little friends!

THE APPLE TREE
Olivia | Age 9

There is a giant apple tree,
right behind my house,
but all it does is sit there,
quiet as a mouse.

It doesn't throw, it doesn't catch,
It won't play a game of chess,
And when it drops its apples,
It makes ME clean up its mess.

But one part is great about it,
So I won't let out a sigh,
the part that is so great about it:
Mom makes us apple pie.

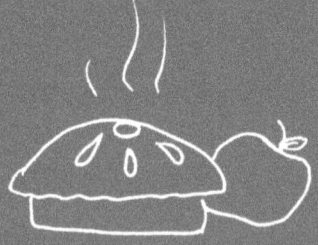

LISTEN
Olivia | Age 12

You ask me why I'm so strange
You ask me why I never change

I could yell the reason
I could scream and shout
But you never stay long enough
To hear me out

Nobody ever listens
Nobody ever hears
The thing that's most important
Suddenly disappears

And no one ever notices
That I'm standing right there
Everybody's in their own world
And they don't seem to care

It's like being in a big huge city
With nowhere to walk to
It's like being at a crowded party
With no one to talk to.

BIRTHDAY POEM FOR GRANDPA
Olivia | Age 17

There's a man who says "the time has come to talk of many things"
There's a man who evaluates the lyrics that one sings
There's a man who drinks his chocolate shake at the end of the day
There's a man who wins every game he does (or doesn't) play.

There's a man who really, REALLY likes to watch the news
There's a man who can take a hint — he does not need clues
There's a man who holds a ledger for everything I owe
There's a man that seems to have learned everything there is to know.

This man has been there for me since the day that I was born
This man is the one and only Minnie Slobbertosh — Whoops,
I mean Morris Corn.

HAPPY BIRTHDAY GRANDPA

Olivia | Age 22

Grandpa Morris is 92 today
And as tradition goes
We will present him with a poem
The art form he best knows.

Grandpa Morris is intelligent,
His smarts beyond compare
He knows his facts; he's quick on his feet
Argue with him if you dare!

Grandpa Morris is quite funny
Always ready with a joke
Like his insistence on our hunger
Or his reminder not to smoke.

But most of all, Grandpa is kind
His love can conquer all
He's always there to make us smile
And catch us if we fall.

So happy birthday Grandpa
We wish you happiness and cheer
We wish you love, and health,
and lots of joy
In your 92nd year.
Love, Olivia

PHANTOM
Olivia | Age 11

I started getting worried
When I scratched my head in thought
And felt a surge of pain
That could not be fought.

And when I touched my elbow
To show mom all my cuts
It started hurting even more
No ifs, ands or buts.

When the school band was playing
I drummed my fingers on my knees
It felt like I'd been attacked
By a mob of swarming bees.

So I went to the doctor
And told him the tale
He checked me head to toe
And reported without fail,

That from the scratching and the cuts
All the way to the stinger
I had a case
Of an awfully broken finger.

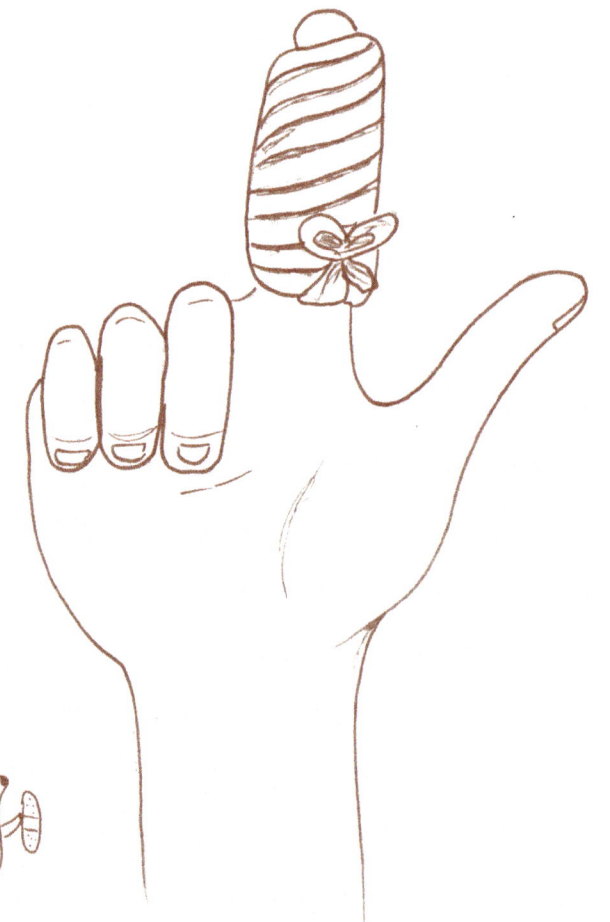

HAPPY BIRTHDAY MOM

Olivia | Age 8

Friends appear, friends disappear
   Some go far, some stay near
      Some friends, you'll find, end up different than before
         But there are some friends who you always will adore.

      Some friends become mean
         And some stay kind
            Those that drift away
               Will stay put in your mind.

         Some friends let go
            Some friends hold on
               But your Mom will be your friend
               For forever on.

                   HAPPY BIRTHDAY, MOM

MORRIS THE CAT — PSSST!
Grandpa Morris

Morris the Cat was a familiar television ad
He was both chunky and fat
His size was an eye opener
To other cats.

It didn't bother Morris
That his owner could no longer
Hold him on his lap.
Morris scared the daylights
Out of the biggest rats.

Great sales pitch
Wouldn't you say?
Although his hairs were everywhere
All things being equal
Grandpa Morris didn't really care.

I AM A PICKY EATER
Olivia | Age 7

I am a picky eater
I don't like pickles, peas, or pears
When I say I don't like it,
No one really cares.

Ice pops make me shiver
Frog legs make me squirm
I won't eat a gum drop or a gummy worm.

All those things I mentioned
I must admit I really lied
All those things I mentioned
I never really tried.

GOING TO BED
Olivia | Age 7

For me going to bed is boring
So while Mom and Dad are snoring
I'll climb into the attic.
Mom said the heat is so hot in there
her hair becomes very static.

It didn't matter to me for sure
cause there are lots of other things in store.

I opened a chest.
Inside there were lots of enchanting things
like crowns and books of gold
And shiny gold rings

But best of all in the corner,
An angel with delicate gold wings.

MICHAEL JAMES

Olivia | Age 7

I know a boy Michael James
He likes beetles, bats and snakes.
He likes throwing paper bags into cold blue lakes.

He put a frog in my lunch box, a lizard in my hair,
And he puts bats and snakes everywhere.

So you can see he's naughty, but he is still my friend.
He will be my friend to the very end.

A DINOSAUR ON MY WALL
Olivia | Age 7

There is a dinosaur on my wall
And it isn't very small.

In fact it is a Tyrannosaurus Rex.
He ate up my toys as quick as a wink.
I wonder what he will do next.

I found out soon enough, because when I was
Looking for my soccer stuff, I saw him eating it all up.
My mother screamed and I beamed when we saw
Him drinking from a dining room cup.

My mother cried and I sighed because he ate up all her pies.
I will be grateful if this dinosaur ever says his goodbyes.

So that is the story of my pet
But I am not finished yet.

I just want to say I'm glad you could come today.

I HAVE A PET

Olivia | Age 7

I have a pet, well not yet
Because I cannot really pick.
I think I'll get a monkey and maybe call him Rick.

No, No, No, a monkey is too crazy and I'm too lazy
To take care of that kind of pet.
So what other pet can I get?

Maybe a polar bear.
I'll tell my parents that I'll swear I will go to the
Arctic by myself and I will get him there.

No, I think I will take it slow,
I'll go to the zoo and maybe get a kangaroo.
Ooh!

IN THE WOODS
Olivia | Age 10

I'm cold (and scared)

I'm freezing

I'm shivering

I'm in a fright

I'm walking through the dark dark woods

In the full moon's light

The woods are dark and I am so scared

When the wolves howl I wish I was spared

I'm shivering so much — It's so cold and so scary

So I have to be oh so wary

FLOWERS
Olivia | Age 10

Blue and yellow, pink and white, oh how I love to see your sight.
You are blooming in spring air,
buds are bursting everywhere.

Blue and yellow, pink and green, you add beauty to the scene.
You are like sunshine, warm and bright,
and midnight moons during the night.

You scent the air like sweet perfume, if we'll let you grow,
we'll give you room.

Flowers

One of the prettiest things on earth.

LOVE
Grandpa Morris

Mary had a little lamb
Looked like a little bear
Every time it growled
People held their breath and stared.

What could Mary do
To straighten out this fear?
Try dipping it in vanilla ice cream
That would dye it's curly hair.

NOT A GOOD IDEA!!!

How about whipped cream
A flavor popular that year?
Everything is really to naught, she thought
What the heck, I have a little bear
That will make me popular everywhere.

And so
Everywhere that Mary went
The bear was sure to go.

SNEEZE LOUISE
Grandpa Morris

Sneezing is an act of grace
As long as you don't sneeze in someone's face.
When you get a sudden itch, count to ten
Go for your handkerchief.
Some sneeze with a heavy stroke
Those sneezes are known as a joke.

The louder the noise the better the grade
When you go to school you've got it made
Everyone will avoid you like the bubonic plague.
Holding one's nose gives some people a fear
If it's contagious, don't sit next to that dear.

Holding your breath and not turning blue
It's not worth the effort
Sneeze.....kerchoo.
Just for the books, some sneezes are long
Finishing like a song.
What's your take ..... right or wrong?

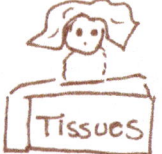

MINNIE SLOBBER TOOTH
Grandpa Morris

Minnie Slobber Tooth was quite a gal
Sweet as pie, with a honey mix
You wouldn't believe that name would stick.

She was blessed with everything else
You could comprehend
Everyone wanted to be her friend.

But for the name ...
Minnie "Slobber Tooth" was an
Embarrassment they claimed.

Change the Name!
Keep everything else the same!

Finally consenting
Minnie Slobber Tooth changed her name
To
Minnie Kitzletoe.

Oh! Ok! What the heck, they said.
We're always your friend —
　we've got your back!

ABBA DABBA DOO
Grandpa Morris

Abba Dabba Doo
Better known as boo, hoo, hoo
Who knew he would become so
Famous as you—
A hug and a squeeze maybe both a thrill—
Especially when the results are true
And the world looks up to you
Your rules are true
Like Abba Dabba Doo
I can use some help too,
Abba Dabba Doo, an illiterate to
The World he knew
So please come through
Abba Dabba Doo is clueless
Come forward and let's see you
His problem to date is dotting his 'i's
And crossing his 't's
So please help him, Please!!!!
Looks like he is crossing his fingers
And stubbing his toes
What do you think? The problem
Can drive you to drink
You think it would be easy
Just to get him in sync
Just to dot his 'i's and cross his 't's in a blink—
It's not all a bluff—
Just crazy stuff

JIMMEY MARCO
Olivia | Age 8

Jimmey Marco bragged about all the things he knew.

He knew about bears,
raccoons,
bats,
whales,
and leopards too.

He knew about leaves,
flowers,
sharks,
and lions ... whew.

He knows about most anything,
artists and movies too.

The only thing he doesn't know
is what is two plus two.

MORRIS NOT HORACE

Grandpa Morris

Why Morris?
What a fabulous name —
Everlasting, catchy, and carries the burden of fame.

Examples are ample —
Morris the Cat for instance sold more food on television
and that was a fact.
Finicky, yes, but so are all cats.

Morris the Moose tickled kids' funny bones loose
Made the NY Times best seller list repeatedly beating Dr. Suess.

Good Lord we are not finished yet, oh yeah!
You got it Grandpa Morris, you bet.

Grandpa Morris not withstanding a fault
Morris by name is tastier than salt.

So 12 cents please, he's always broke
but good for a laugh
and a joke.

ODE TO A HUG AND A SQUEEZE
Grandpa Morris

Grandpa Morris needs a hug and a squeeze
Grandma Ruth makes him pick up the crumbs after he eats

Grandpa Morris needs a hug and a squeeze
His chocolate bar melted and is no longer a treat

Grandpa Morris needs a hug and a squeeze
His poetry skills left him in a deep freeze

Grandpa Morris needs a hug and a squeeze
His checker board game is just a big tease

Grandpa Morris needs a hug and a squeeze
Even nap time has not been a breeze

ANYBODY—PLEASE
GRANDPA MORRIS DESPERATELY NEEDS
A HUG AND A SQUEEZE!!!!!!!!!

POET TO POET
Grandpa Morris

Olivia, your memory is quite outstanding
Great recall has my heart pounding

Your recollections, an amazing image
Of my wonderful sayings, collected and finished

They have proven to be of the highest loft
So let's keep the game and sayings soft

Whisper them in the family tree
Remember 12 cents is a small fee
Kudos for my legacy.

OLIVIA MICHELLE

Grandpa Morris

Olivia Michelle may she thrive and grow
Has a head on her shoulders smarter than any nine-year-old I know.

Her beautiful blond hair is an eye catcher I'm told
Her speech is explicit, her vocabulary bold.

Her checker playing needs work after Grandpa takes a nap
Because then he's sharp and stays on track.

Olivia Michelle's poetry writing gives Grandpa a scare
He can't seem to compete or even get near.

To her sister Cayla she is untiringly sweet
All in all this summation is quite complete.

So thank you Olivia for being my granddaughter
She knows she deserves the praise I accord her.

I CAN TAKE A HINT

Grandpa Morris

When someone says wipe your nose
I can take a hint

When someone says
There's a stain on your shirt
I can take a hint

When someone says pass the salt
Is there a please there
I can take a hint

When someone says stop talking
I can take a hint

When someone says don't squint
I can take a hint

When someone says
You're annoying
I can take a hint

When someone says
You need a haircut
I can take a hint

When someone says
Wipe your mouth
I can take a hint

Stop!
You would never know with these sayings
that I am really a saint!
I am blessed — I can take a hint.

NO YOU CAN'T!

I AM
Michelle Leah, a family friend | Age 12

I am a rare red rose in a meadow of sunflowers. I paint my world with vibrant colors, and search for my pot of gold at the end of each rainbow. I take risks and walk through the threshold of every door that I stumble upon. I am a train racing down the tracks of life and I care for the passengers that I bring along with me. I write the story of my life with my dreams waiting to be added as a new chapter in my journey through this universe. I am a baby bird anxious to spread its wings and fly, ready to make its mark on the world. I make mistakes and I'm not perfect but, I am perfect at doing the job I was born with, and that is being me.

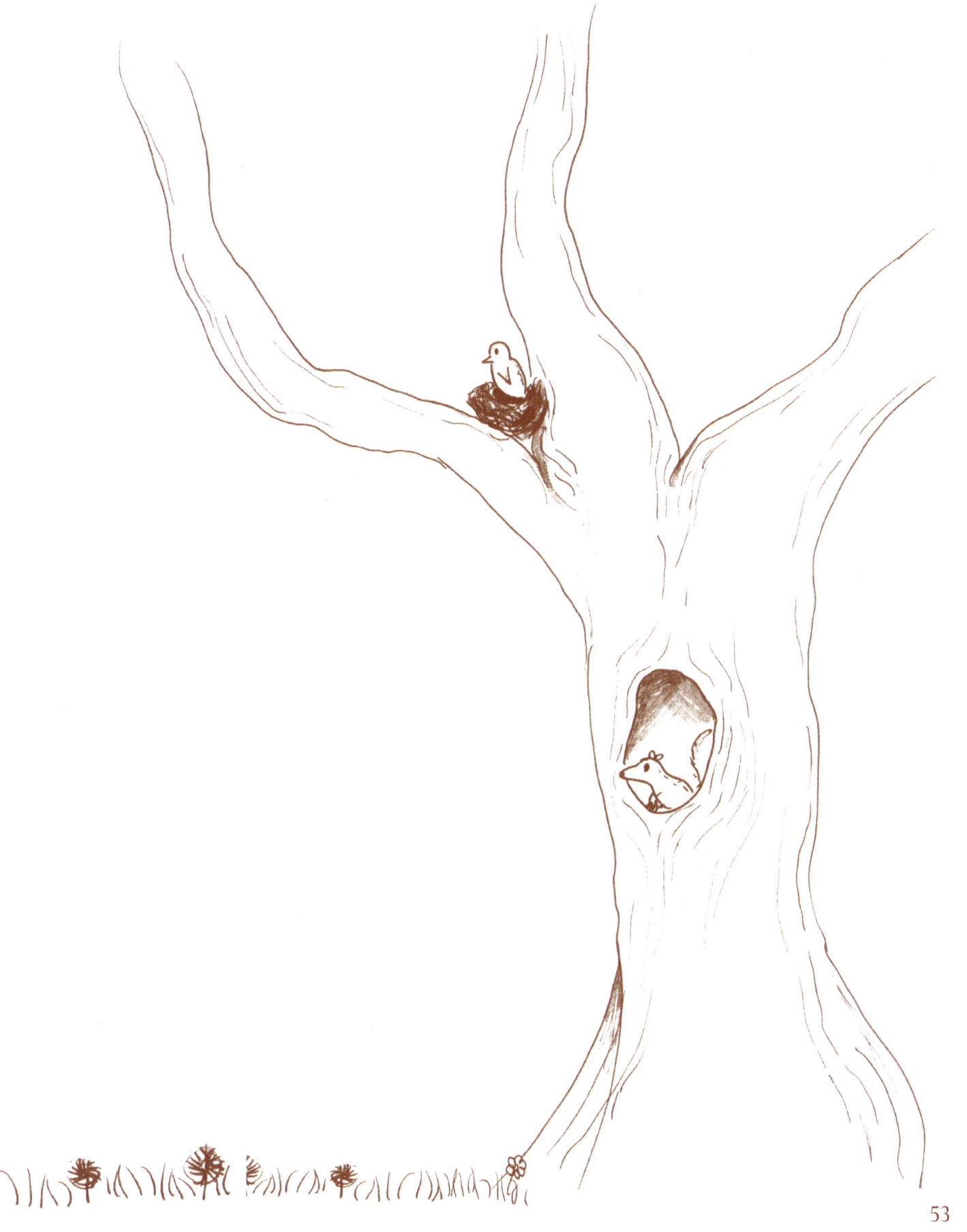

Morris Corn wrote this poem before he was a grandpa, when he was a sophomore at Paterson State Teacher's College, where the poem won a collegiate award. Grandpa Morris has loved writing poetry for a long time!

KEATS
Morris Corn | 1950

O Keats, the sages pen of you has writ,

O Keats, no greater memory is vast

Be Keats, eternity the poet past

On Death — On Solitude — On Peace, Keats knit.

Love — beauty — truth, inspired fiery wit,

O Keats, given immortality thou hast,

Associates to future ages cast,

O Keats, nature in you a flame alit,

Be sober, Keats hast made earth benefit

Thrill beat his poetry made life here last

O blackened cloud — thunder — thunder — louder,

Rain-drops, Rain-drops, sprinkle earth abit.

From GODS inspir'd creative genius hast,

Departed Keats, a bud matured a flower.

WHAT IS POETRY?

- A limerick is a humorous poem consisting of 5 lines
- A ballad is a poem or song narrating a story in short stanzas
- Free verse is an open form of poetry:
  - Poetry that does or does not rhyme
  - Does or does not have a regular meter
- The Sonnet is a 14-line poem with a variable rhyme scheme
- Lyric verse is a formal type of poetry which expresses personal emotions or feelings typically spoken in the first person:
  - A short highly musical verse that conveys powerful feelings
  - Poet may use rhyme, meter, or other literary devices to create a song-like quality
- An Ode is a lyric poem usually marked by exaltation of feeling and style, varying length of line and complexity of stanza forms
- Nonsense Verse is a rhyme that prompts laughter

לְדוֹר וָדוֹר
"L'DOR V'DOR"

There is a saying in Hebrew — L'dor v'dor — which literally means "from generation to generation." It is understood to mean the transmission of the culture's values, rituals, traditions, and history to the next generation.

This collection of poems is a love for poetry passed "l'dor v'dor" — "from generation to generation" — from Grandfather to Granddaughter.

Morris Corn's first class (6th grade) in 1952 in the Upper Saddle River School System, where he first introduced "The Walrus and the Carpenter" by Lewis Carroll.

The Upper Saddle River School System was one of the last one-room schoolhouses in Bergen County, NJ, with K-8 taught in one classroom, by one teacher. The school moved to a new, 4-room building shown in this photo. Classes were half-day sessions due to a shortage of classroom space. Morris Corn shared his sixth-grade classroom with the kindergarten class.

At 22, as a new teacher in the 6th grade, Morris Corn introduced poetry to his students, making it integral to his curriculum. Over the years, when he met former students, they often recited a poem they learned with him in the sixth grade, which shows — poetry means so much and stays with you forever.

Later, Morris Corn became the first Principal of Upper Saddle River's newly built K-3 primary school, the Robert D. Reynolds Elementary School.

Commemorative plate picturing the original Upper Saddle River School System one-room schoolhouse.

Artist's rendering of current Robert D. Reynolds Elementary School

At his retirement as Principal, after 39 years of service for the Upper Saddle River School System, the teachers presented Dr. Corn with this copy of "The Walrus and the Carpenter." It is his favorite poem and one that all of his 6th grade students loved as well and came to know by heart!

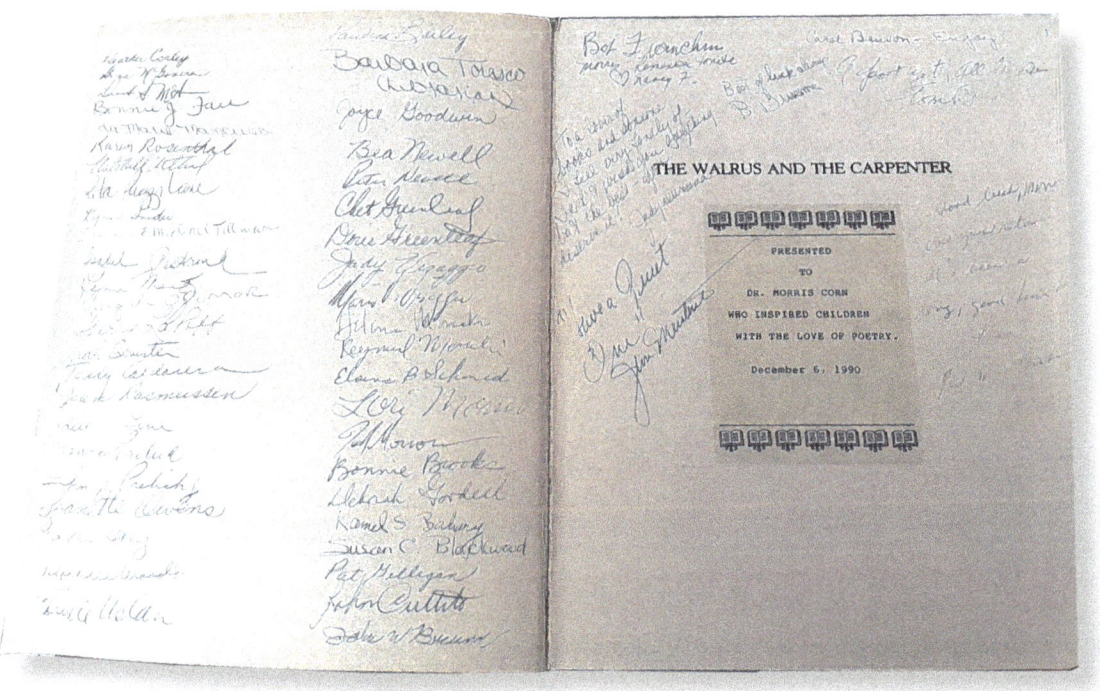

Book signed by all of Dr. Corn's teachers (pictured below) at Robert D. Reynolds Elementary School.

Original copy of "The Squirrel" written by Olivia at age 10.

For Grandpa

The Squirrel

I was sitting
At the table
When outside
I saw a squirrel
On a tree.
It jumped
Onto a branch
That was thin.
The branch shook
Under the squirrel.
    UP and
        DOWN
      UP and
    Down.
I covered my eyes
I was sure
It would fall.
BUT
It did not.
It scampered
Off the branch
And went
To a higher one.
The same thing
happened.
again.
And again
And again.
Until it fell.
It was
A long
    way
        down.
BUT
    It did not die.
The squirrel tried
again.
Because a squirrel
knows
not
to
give
up.
Even though
It's just a squirrel.

Olivia (age 4)

Olivia (age 6)

Olivia (age 8) and Cayla
(the "Little Companion")

Olivia (age 10) reading her poem
"Ode to a Grandpa" at Grandpa's
80th birthday celebration

Olivia (age 13) and Cayla

Poetry Contest Night — Olivia (age 8), Grandpa, Cayla, Kim (Olivia's mom) and Noah (grandson)

Noah, Nate (grandsons), Cayla and Olivia (age 9) creating together

Grandpa with grandchildren Michaela (age 10), Becky (age 6), Kevin (age 4) reading "The Walrus and the Carpenter" by Lewis Caroll

Grandpa and Olivia (age 7 and 19)

Time together:
Olivia (age 6, 7, 8, 9, and 14; clockwise from the top left) and Grandpa

Celebrating Grandpa's birthdays

The Corn family

The authors hard at work on *Two Poets and a Squirrel.*

ABOUT THE AUTHORS

Dr. Morris Corn is a former day camp director and owner, sixth grade teacher, elementary school Principal, education curriculum developer, and restauranteur. He has been recognized statewide and nationally for his innovative programming both in education and recreation. Under his fun, creative, and passionate leadership, his elementary school repeatedly placed in the highest, national educational rankings. He is the proud father of five children, twelve grandchildren and nine great-grandchildren. He is an avid reader and loves history and political science. Dr. Corn is admired and adored by his family, friends, and colleagues alike. He currently resides in Delray Beach, Florida with Ruth, his loving and patient wife of sixty-nine years. As for his love for his family and friends, Dr. Corn says, "my cup runneth over."

Olivia Michelle is 24 years old. She has always enjoyed writing, since an early age. Through weekly writing with Grandpa, school, local, and national competitions, winning scholastic art and writing awards, serving on her high school newspaper, and her own personal writing projects, Olivia has cultivated her passion. She is excited to share it with others through *Two Poets and a Squirrel* and is incredibly honored to have her poems printed beside her grandfather's. Olivia graduated with her bachelor's degree from Lafayette College in 2022, with a major in International Affairs and minor in Environmental Studies. With a passion for helping others, during her four years at Lafayette she was a member of the Refugee Action club, and post college, spent a year working at the International Rescue Committee in New York City. Olivia is currently earning her master's in Public Policy at Duke University.

ABOUT THE ILLUSTRATORS

Kelsey DeVries is 19 years old. She developed an interest for drawing at the age of 8 and since then has fallen in love with all different types of art. She feels very honored to have worked alongside Morris Corn and his family in creating this project and is excited for it to be shared. She is currently studying accountancy in her sophomore year at Providence College.

Nate Frank is 20 years old and Dr. Corn's grandson. From a very young age, Nate has studied a variety of art forms, including drawing, painting, watercolors, graphic design, and photography; his work was showcased at the town library. Nate loved being a part of this book with Grandpa and Olivia. He's been listening to, laughing, and loving his grandfather's creative storytelling for as long as he can remember, including "The Squirrel with a Runny Nose" and "Meanwhile Back at the Ranch..." Nate is currently a junior at Bates College studying psychology, art, and marketing.

ACKNOWLEDGEMENTS

I have enjoyed working with and teaching children all my adult life, so putting together Olivia's and my poetry came naturally. I thank my wife Ruth, for her encouragement and clinical review to keep the project alive.

I give special thanks to: my daughter Kim, who spent so much time at the library and at the copy machine making sure the book would fit the market; my daughter Joni, who handled the legal aspects of the project as well the order and rhythm of the book; my son-in-law Tim, who served as literary consultant; my son Andre gets a special thank you for working so closely with me on compiling and printing pages and pictures for this book; my daughter Shara and son Marc, who provided loving encouragement; my artists, Kelsie and my grandson Nate, who turned Olivia's and my words into captivating images; and my graphic designer, Meher, who cared so much and laid it all out into a beautiful book and a work of art. This poetry book would not have happened were it not for my good friend Tom Sheridan who made things happen when they were at a stand still. A thank you to all my family members who have spent so much time contributing to this effort.

It is my hope that in the years ahead, literature classes will read these poems and promote children's literature and the love of poetry as much as Olivia and I have enjoyed it. I feel privileged to share with all children. All in all, my family and friends are the kindred spirits to whom I owe this debt of gratitude.

A few poems in this book reference lines from the following verse of "The Walrus and the Carpenter" by Lewis Carroll. Grandpa Morris frequently quotes them in real life, and thus they are found in poems about him or by him. Proper credit is given here:

> "The time has come," the Walrus said,
>   To talk of many things:
> Of shoes - and ships - and sealing-wax -
>   of cabbages - and kings -
> And why the sea is boiling hot -
>   And whether pigs have wings."

"Braggy Bart" mentions "...shoes, or ships, or sealing wax"
"Birthday Poem for Grandpa" mentions "...the time has come to talk of many things..."

Publisher's Cataloging-in-Publication Data

Names: Corn, Morris, author. | Michelle, Olivia, author. | DeVries, Kelsey, illustrator. | Frank, Nate, illustrator.

Title: Two poets and a squirrel : a poetry collection that inspires , connects , and celebrates multigenerational bonding / by Morris Corn, EdD and Olivia Michelle; illustrated by Nate Frank and Kelsey DeVries.

Description: Delray Beach, FL: Corn Generation Link, 2024. | Summary: A collection of poems spanning 15 years, capturing the playful and heartfelt exchanges between Grandpa Morris and his granddaughter, Olivia.

Identifiers: LCCN: 2024914939 | ISBN: 979-8-9910245-1-8 (hardcover) | 979-8-9910245-0-1 (paperback) | 979-8-9910245-2-5 (ebook)

Subjects: LCSH American poetry--21st century. | Children's poetry, American. | BISAC JUVENILE FICTION / Poetry

Classification: LCC PZ7.1 .C67 Two 2024 | DDC 811.6--dc23

INDEX OF POEMS

A

A DINOSAUR ON MY WALL, 36
ABBA DABA DOO, 45
AN ODE BY GRANDPA, 22

B

BIRTHDAY POEM FOR GRANDPA, 28
BRAGGY BART, 23
BUILD ME UP, 21

F

FLOWERS, 40

G

GOING TO BED, 34
GRANDPA MORRIS' FAMOUS
  HANDSHAKE, 14

H

HAPPY BIRTHDAY GRANDPA, 29
HAPPY BIRTHDAY MOM, 31

I

I AM, 52
I AM A PICKY EATER, 33
I CAN TAKE A HINT, 51
I HAVE A PET, 37
IN THE WOODS, 38

J

JIMMEY MARCO, 46

K

KEATS, 55

L

LISTEN, 27
LITTLE JAMIE'S BLANKET, 13
LOVE, 41
LUCK, 15

M

MICHAEL JAMES, 35
MINNIE SLOBBER TOOTH, 43
MORRIS NOT HORACE, 47
MORRIS THE CAT — PSSST!, 32
MY FATHER'S CREDIT CARD, 12
MY LITTLE COMPANION, 20

O

ODE TO A GRANDPA, 8
ODE TO A HUG AND A SQUEEZE, 48
OLIVIA'S ALMOST 11, 9
OLIVIA MICHELLE, 50

P

PHANTOM, 30
POEM #1, 18
POEM #2, 19
POEM NUMBER 3A, 16
POEM NUMBER 3B, 17
POET TO POET, 49

S

SNEEZE LOUISE, 42

T

THE APPLE TREE, 24
THE BABYSITTER, 11
THE SQUIRREL, 7

W

WHY DOES MY TEACHER HATE ME?, 10

WRITE, DRAW, EXPLORE...

www.ingramcontent.com/pod-product-compliance
Lightning Source LLC
Chambersburg PA
CBHW042012060526
44119CB00114B/283